About the Author

Meet the author - a seasoned technology executive with over 20 years of experience, a self-directed approach, and an unwavering passion for quality, reliability, and continuous improvement. Having worked globally across diverse industries such as Banking, FMCG, Retail, Manufacturing, Hospitality, Food & Beverage, Education, and Construction in SSA, EMEA, and APAC regions, I have developed a highly skilled and adaptable mindset that prioritizes critical thinking and innovation.

With expertise in Digital Transformation, IT infrastructure, Software Development, Cyber Security, IT operational excellence and Technology project management, I have a proven track record of executing strategic plans and delivering efficient outcomes. I take pride in building and inspiring high-

1

performance teams through collaboration, inclusion, and passionate leadership.

In this book, I delve into the pitfalls and opportunities of Digital Transformation in business, drawing from my extensive experience to provide insights and practical solutions to navigate this complex and rapidly evolving landscape. I hope you find this short summary informative and engaging.

Contents

Chapter 1: Pitfalls of Digital Transformation and How to Avoid Them

While the benefits of digital transformation are clear, it is not without its challenges and potential pitfalls. Many organizations have embarked on digital transformation initiatives, only to find themselves facing unexpected roadblocks or failing to achieve the desired outcomes.

Research suggests that digital transformation projects have a relatively low success rate. Only about 16% of digital transformation projects achieve their goals fully.

The purpose of this book is to provide guidance on how to avoid the potential pitfalls of digital transformation and emerge as a leader in the fast-paced digital economy. I will examine case studies of both successful and unsuccessful digital transformations, and provide practical guidance on how to avoid common pitfalls and apply best practices for successful digital transformation.

Chapter 2: Defining Digital Transformation

In recent years, the term digital transformation has become a ubiquitous buzzword, if not a cliché by now. From small startups to large multinational corporations, every organization seems to be talking about digital transformation. But what exactly does it mean and why do so many digital transformation projects fail?

At its core, digital transformation refers to the integration of digital technologies into all aspects of an organization's operations, processes, and strategies. This integration can enable organizations to improve efficiency, increase agility, and enhance customer experiences, ultimately leading to increased competitiveness and profitability.

The digital technologies that are driving this transformation can take many forms, including cloud-based computing, data analytics, artificial intelligence, machine learning, automation, and the Internet of Things (IoT). These technologies have the potential to fundamentally change how organizations operate and create value for their stakeholders.

However, digital transformation is not just about implementing new technologies. It also involves a cultural shift within the organization to embrace new ways of working, collaboration, and decision-making. This shift requires a willingness to take risks, experiment, and learn from failures.

At its core, digital transformation is about leveraging technology to create a more agile, innovative, and customer-centric organization. By embracing digital transformation, organizations can gain a competitive advantage by responding more quickly to market changes, improving operational efficiency, and creating more personalized and engaging experiences for their customers.

In the following chapters, I will explore the potential benefits of digital transformation, and even more importantly I will also explore the potential pitfalls and challenges that organizations may face along the way. I will examine case studies of both successful and unsuccessful digital transformations, and provide guidance on how to avoid common pitfalls and best practices for successful digital transformation. Ultimately, my goal is to help organizations navigate the complex world of digital transformation and emerge as leaders in the fast-paced digital economy.

We can ask ourselves the question: "What is driving the current focus on digital transformation at this moment in time. Why has digital transformation come to the fore in the recent past number of years?"

The COVID-19 pandemic has been a major catalyst for the focus on digital transformation across many industries. As lockdowns and social distancing measures were implemented, businesses had to quickly adapt to remote work and digital communication. This forced many companies to accelerate their digital transformation efforts to stay operational and competitive in a rapidly changing business environment.

In addition, the pandemic has also shifted consumer behavior towards digital channels. With brick-and-mortar stores closed or limited in capacity, consumers turned to online shopping and digital services, such as telemedicine and online education. This has further emphasized the importance of digital transformation for businesses to meet the evolving needs of their customers.

Furthermore, advancements in technology such as cloud computing, artificial intelligence, and the Internet of Things have made digital transformation more accessible and cost-effective for businesses of all sizes. These technologies have become more commoditized that ever before. These technologies have enabled new business models and opportunities that were cost-prohibitive before.

Overall, the COVID-19 pandemic, changing consumer behavior, and advancements in technology have created a perfect storm that has pushed many businesses to prioritize digital transformation as a key strategic initiative.

Chapter 3: The Importance of Digital Transformation in Modern Business

In today's fast-paced and constantly evolving business world, digital transformation has become essential for organizations to remain competitive and relevant. The benefits of digital transformation are numerous, and failure to embrace it can lead to being left behind in the market.

Improved Efficiency and Cost Savings Driving Improved Margins

Digital transformation has the potential to significantly improve efficiency and cost savings for businesses, thereby improving operating margins. On the other hand, new digital channels that make the customers more accessible than before, help increase top-line revenue. By automating manual processes, digitizing documents, and leveraging data analytics, businesses can streamline operations, reduce errors, and save time. For example, implementing digital workflows can eliminate the need for manual approvals and paperwork, reducing processing times and minimizing the risk of errors. Digitizing documents can also reduce storage costs and improve accessibility, as documents can be easily retrieved and shared electronically.

In addition, digital transformation can help businesses better understand their customers and operations through data analytics. By analyzing customer behavior and operational data, businesses can identify areas for improvement and optimize their processes for better efficiency. This can also lead to cost savings by reducing waste, improving inventory management, and optimizing supply chain processes.

Overall, digital transformation can drive improved efficiency and cost savings by automating processes, digitizing documents, and leveraging data analytics. By optimizing operations and reducing costs, businesses can become more competitive and better equipped to succeed in today's digital economy.

Here's an example of how digital transformation can lead to improved efficiency and cost savings: Let's consider a traditional retail store that manually tracks its inventory, sales, and customer data on paper or spreadsheets. This process is time-consuming and prone to errors, which can lead to stockouts, overstocking, and inefficiencies in supply chain management.

However, with the adoption of digital tools such as inventory management software, point-of-sale systems, and customer relationship management (CRM) software, the store can significantly improve its efficiency and reduce costs.

For example, an inventory management system can automatically track stock levels, reorder products when inventory falls below a certain threshold, and provide real-time data on product performance. This eliminates the need for manual inventory tracking, reduces the risk of stockouts, and minimizes overstocking.

Similarly, a point-of-sale system can streamline the checkout process, reduce human error, and provide real-time sales data that can inform inventory decisions.

Finally, a CRM system can automate marketing and sales activities, improve customer engagement, and provide insights into customer behavior, preferences, and buying patterns. This can help the store personalize its offerings, improve customer satisfaction, and increase sales.

Overall, by embracing digital transformation, the retail store can improve its efficiency, reduce costs, and enhance the customer experience, leading to increased profitability and growth.

Enhanced Customer Experience Driving Revenue Increase

Another critical benefit of digital transformation is enhanced customer experience. Digital technologies allow organizations to create more personalized and engaging experiences for their customers, which can help build brand loyalty and increase customer retention.

Here is a well-known example from the banking industry explaining how digital transformation improved customer experience: Let's consider a traditional brick-and-mortar bank that relies on face-to-face interactions to provide customer service. While this approach has its merits, it can be time-consuming and inconvenient for customers who need to visit the bank during business hours.

However, by adopting digital tools such as online banking, mobile banking, and chatbots, the bank can significantly enhance its customer experience.

For example, online banking allows customers to access their accounts 24/7, check their balance, view transaction history, and transfer funds from the comfort of their own homes. This eliminates the need for customers to physically visit the bank and reduces wait times.

Similarly, mobile banking allows customers to perform these same tasks from their mobile devices, making banking even more convenient and accessible.

Finally, chatbots can provide customers with instant assistance, answering frequently asked questions and directing customers to the right resources. This can improve the bank's responsiveness and reduce the need for customers to wait on hold for a representative.

Overall, by embracing digital transformation, the bank can enhance its customer experience, providing convenience, accessibility, and responsiveness that meet the needs of today's tech-savvy customers.

Chapter 4: The Importance of Customer Experience in Driving Revenue Growth

4.1 Definition of Customer Experience

Customer experience has always been an essential aspect of business success. It refers to the overall experience a customer has with a brand or business, from initial awareness to post-purchase follow-up. A great customer experience is crucial to building customer loyalty, driving repeat business, and attracting new customers through positive word-of-mouth.

With the rise of digital technologies, the customer experience landscape has changed significantly. In the context of digital transformation, customer experience refers to the integration of digital technologies, such as mobile apps, social media, websites, chatbots, and others, into every aspect of the customer journey.

Digital transformation has revolutionized customer experience by making it more personalized, efficient, and convenient. It allows businesses to gain a deeper understanding of their customers' needs and preferences through data analytics and AI-powered insights. This, in turn, enables them to provide tailored solutions, personalized recommendations, and proactive support, resulting in a more satisfying customer experience.

At the heart of digital transformation is the need for businesses to be customer-centric. This means understanding the customer journey and the touchpoints where digital technologies can enhance the customer experience. For example, a business can use data analytics to identify customer pain points and use this information to improve the customer experience at those specific touchpoints.

Personalization is another key aspect of the digital customer experience. Customers expect businesses to know their preferences, interests, and behavior and to use this information to provide personalized recommendations, content, and offers. Personalization can be achieved through data analytics, AI-powered recommendation engines, and chatbots that use natural language processing to understand customer needs and provide relevant solutions.

Another essential aspect of digital transformation in customer experience is omnichannel integration. Customers expect a seamless experience across all channels, including social media, websites, mobile apps, and physical stores. An omnichannel approach requires businesses to integrate data and communication channels, providing a consistent experience across all touchpoints.

However, digital transformation also presents challenges for customer experience, such as data privacy concerns, security risks, and the need for seamless integration across various digital channels. Therefore, successful digital transformation requires businesses to prioritize customer-centricity and invest in the right technologies and processes to ensure a seamless and secure digital customer experience.

Data privacy and security are critical considerations for digital customer experience. Customers want to know that their personal information is protected and that businesses are using it only to provide relevant and personalized experiences. Therefore, businesses must implement secure data management and cybersecurity protocols to protect customer data.

Furthermore, businesses must ensure that digital technologies are integrated seamlessly across all channels. A disjointed customer experience can be frustrating for customers and result in negative perceptions of the brand. Therefore, businesses must invest in the right technologies and processes to ensure a smooth and consistent customer experience across all touchpoints.

Digital transformation has transformed the customer experience landscape by providing businesses with new opportunities to personalize, optimize, and enhance the customer journey. However, it also presents challenges that businesses must address to ensure a seamless and secure digital customer experience. The key to successful digital transformation in customer experience is prioritizing customer-centricity, investing in the right technologies and processes, and staying up-to-date with the latest trends and best practices in digital transformation.

4.2 The Link between Customer Experience and Revenue Growth

Studies have shown that there is a direct link between customer experience and revenue growth. Businesses that provide superior customer experience are more likely to attract and retain customers, which can lead to increased sales and revenue growth. A report by Forrester found that companies that prioritize customer experience grow their revenue at a rate of 5.1 times that of companies that don't prioritize customer experience.

4.3 The Role of Digital Transformation in Enhancing Customer Experience

Digital transformation has revolutionized the way businesses interact with their customers. By leveraging digital technologies, businesses can provide a personalized, convenient, and fast experience that meets the specific needs and preferences of their customers. Digital technologies such as big data analytics, artificial intelligence, and the internet of things (IoT) can provide valuable insights into customer behavior and preferences, enabling businesses to provide personalized experiences that drive customer loyalty and revenue growth.

Chapter 5: How Digital Transformation Enhances Customer Experience

5.1 Personalization

One of the key benefits of digital transformation is the ability to provide personalized experiences to customers. By collecting and analyzing customer data, businesses can gain insights into their customers' preferences and behavior, enabling them to offer personalized products and services. Personalization can drive customer loyalty and repeat business, which can lead to increased revenue growth.

For example, Amazon uses customer data to provide personalized product recommendations and targeted advertising. By analyzing customers' purchase histories and browsing behavior, Amazon can suggest products that customers are more likely to be interested in purchasing. This personalization improves the customer experience, increasing the likelihood of repeat purchases and driving revenue growth.

5.2 Convenience

Digital transformation can make it easier for customers to interact with businesses and make purchases. By providing convenient, 24/7 access to products and services, businesses can improve customer satisfaction, drive repeat purchases, and increase revenue.

For example, companies like Uber and Lyft have transformed the transportation industry by providing an easy and convenient way for customers to request and pay for rides. These services offer customers the ability to request a ride at any time of day, from anywhere, and pay through a mobile app. This convenience improves the customer experience, increasing the likelihood of repeat business and driving revenue growth.

5.3 Speed

Digital transformation can speed up business processes and reduce the time it takes to deliver products and services to customers. This can result in faster response times, improved customer satisfaction, and increased revenue.

For example, online retailers like Amazon and Walmart have implemented same-day or next-day delivery services, which have transformed the retail industry. These fast delivery times improve the customer experience, increasing the likelihood of repeat purchases and driving revenue growth.

5.4 Customer Insights

Digital transformation can provide businesses with valuable insights into customer behavior and preferences. By using this information to tailor their products and services, businesses can improve customer satisfaction, increase customer retention, and drive revenue growth.

For example, companies like Netflix and Spotify use customer data to personalize their recommendations for movies, TV shows, and music. By analyzing customers' viewing or listening history, these services can suggest content that customers are more likely to enjoy, improving the customer experience and increasing the likelihood of repeat business.

5.5 Omnichannel Experience

Digital transformation has enabled businesses to provide an omnichannel experience, where customers can interact with the business through multiple channels such as website, mobile app, social media, and physical store. This integrated experience provides customers with a seamless and consistent experience across all touchpoints, which can improve customer satisfaction, increase customer loyalty, and drive revenue growth.

For example, companies like Nike have implemented an omnichannel experience that enables customers to purchase products through the Nike website, mobile app, or physical store. Customers can also use the Nike mobile app to track their fitness progress, receive personalized training plans, and connect with other Nike users. This integrated experience improves the customer experience, increasing the likelihood of repeat purchases and driving revenue growth.

Chapter 6: How Enhanced Customer Experience Drives Revenue Growth and Improved Margins

6.1 Increased Customer Loyalty

Enhanced customer experience can improve customer loyalty, which can lead to increased revenue growth and improved profit margins. Loyal customers are more likely to make repeat purchases, recommend the business to others, and be willing to pay more for the company's products or services.

For example, a study by Harvard Business Review found that customers who had the best past experiences spend 140% more compared to those who had the poorest past experiences. This demonstrates the importance of customer experience in driving revenue growth.

6.2 Reduced Customer Churn

Enhanced customer experience can also reduce customer churn, which can improve profit margins. Customer churn refers to the number of customers who stop using the company's products or services. By improving the customer experience, businesses can reduce customer churn, which can reduce the costs associated with acquiring new customers and improve profit margins.

For example, a study by Bain & Company found that increasing customer retention by just 5% can increase profits by 25% to 95%, depending on the industry. This demonstrates the importance of customer retention in improving profit margins.

6.3 Increased Customer Lifetime Value

Enhanced customer experience can also increase the customer lifetime value (CLV), which is the total revenue that a customer generates for the company over their lifetime. By providing a superior customer experience, businesses can increase the likelihood of repeat purchases and customer loyalty, which can increase the CLV and drive revenue growth.

For example, a study by McKinsey & Company found that customers who are highly satisfied with their experiences with a company are 80% more likely to return to that company for future purchases. This demonstrates the importance of customer satisfaction in driving revenue growth.

6.4 Increased Revenue per Customer

Enhanced customer experience can also increase the revenue per customer, which can improve profit margins. By providing personalized products and services and offering upsells and cross-sells, businesses can increase the average revenue per customer, driving revenue growth and improving profit margins.

For example, a study by Econsultancy found that personalized emails had a 29% higher open rate and a 41% higher click-through rate compared to non-personalized emails. This demonstrates the effectiveness of personalized marketing in driving revenue growth.

Digital transformation has revolutionized the way businesses interact with their customers, enabling them to provide personalized, convenient, and fast experiences that improve customer satisfaction, increase customer loyalty, and drive revenue growth. By leveraging digital technologies such as big data analytics, artificial intelligence, and the internet of things, businesses can gain valuable insights into customer behavior and preferences, enabling them to provide tailored products and services that enhance the customer experience. Enhanced customer experience can drive revenue growth and improve profit margins by increasing customer loyalty, reducing customer churn, increasing customer lifetime value, and increasing revenue per customer. Therefore, businesses that prioritize customer experience.

6.5 The Importance of Data Analytics

With the availability of real-time data and analytics, organizations can better understand their customers' needs and preferences, allowing them to tailor products and services to meet those needs. Data analytics is crucial for improving the customer experience as it provides businesses with valuable insights into customer behavior and preferences. By analyzing customer data, businesses can better understand their customers' needs and preferences, allowing them to tailor their products and services to meet those needs. For example, by analyzing customer feedback and purchase history, businesses can identify patterns and trends in customer behavior, such as preferred products or preferred channels for communication. This can help businesses develop targeted marketing campaigns and personalized offers that resonate with their customers.

Moreover, data analytics can also help businesses anticipate customer needs and proactively address issues before they arise. By analyzing customer data in real-time, businesses can quickly identify and resolve issues, improving customer satisfaction and loyalty. For example, by monitoring social media channels for customer feedback, businesses can identify and address negative comments before they escalate into larger issues.

Overall, data analytics is essential for improving the customer experience by providing businesses with valuable insights into customer behavior and preferences. By leveraging these insights, businesses can develop targeted marketing campaigns, personalized offers, and proactive solutions that meet their customers' needs and expectations, leading to increased customer satisfaction and loyalty.

Here's an example of how data analytics can be used to enhance customer experience: Let's consider an e-commerce website that sells a wide range of products. By collecting and analyzing customer data such as purchase history, browsing behavior, and demographics, the website can gain valuable insights into customer preferences and behavior.

Using these insights, the website can provide personalized recommendations and targeted promotions that are tailored to each customer's interests and needs. For example, if a customer frequently purchases skincare products, the website can recommend related products such as moisturizers, serums, and cleansers. This can improve the customer's shopping experience and increase the likelihood of repeat purchases.

Data analytics can also be used to improve the website's user interface and design. By tracking user behavior such as click-through rates, scroll depth, and time on page, the website can identify areas that need improvement and make data-driven changes. For example, if users are frequently abandoning their shopping carts on a particular page, the website can optimize that page to make it more user-friendly and reduce friction.

Finally, data analytics can be used to measure customer satisfaction and identify areas for improvement. By collecting feedback through surveys or social media, the website can gain insights into customer pain points and take action to address them. For example, if customers are consistently complaining about slow delivery times, the website can work to improve its logistics and shipping processes.

Overall, by leveraging data analytics, the e-commerce website can enhance its customer experience, providing personalized recommendations, optimizing user experience, and improving customer satisfaction.

6.6 Increased Agility and Innovation

Digital transformation can help businesses become more agile and innovative in several ways:

1. Streamlining processes: Digital transformation involves automating and digitizing business processes, which can help eliminate bottlenecks and reduce the time and resources required to complete tasks. This can enable businesses to respond more quickly to changes in the market and customer needs.

2. Data-driven decision making: Digital transformation often involves implementing data analytics tools and techniques to gather insights and make informed decisions. By analyzing data in real-time, businesses can identify trends, detect potential problems, make predictions, and make adjustments quickly to stay ahead of the competition.

3. Increased collaboration and communication: Digital tools such as cloud-based software, video conferencing, and instant messaging can facilitate collaboration and

communication across teams and departments. This can help break down silos and enable teams to work more effectively and efficiently, leading to faster innovation.

4. Greater customer engagement: Digital channels such as social media, mobile apps, and chatbots provide businesses with new ways and an omni-channel approach to engage with customers and gather feedback. By listening to customer needs and preferences, businesses can create products and services that better meet their customers' expectations, leading to increased customer loyalty and retention.

One practical example of how digital transformation can lead to increased agility and innovation is through the use of cloud computing.

Cloud computing enables organizations to access computing resources, such as storage and processing power, over the internet instead of relying on physical hardware located on-premises. This means that companies can quickly scale up or down their computing resources as needed, without having to invest in and manage their own hardware.

As a result, companies can more easily experiment with new ideas and technologies, quickly spinning up new virtual environments to test out new applications or services. This increased agility allows companies to innovate faster, bringing new products and services to market more quickly and responding more rapidly to changing customer needs.

For example, consider a company that wants to develop a new mobile application. With traditional on-premises infrastructure, the company might need to purchase new servers and hardware, install software, and configure the environment before even starting to develop the application. This could take weeks or even months.

With cloud computing, the company can quickly spin up virtual servers and storage, install the necessary software, and begin developing the application almost immediately. As they develop and test the application, they can quickly scale up or down their computing resources as needed to ensure optimal performance.

This increased agility and flexibility enables companies to innovate faster and more efficiently, ultimately leading to increased competitiveness and growth in the marketplace.

Digital transformation has become a key driver for agility and innovation across various industries. Organizations that embrace digital transformation are able to adapt to rapidly changing business landscapes, leverage technological advancements, and create new opportunities for growth and competitive advantage. In this article, I will explore how digital transformation assists agility and innovation in different industries, including finance, healthcare, manufacturing, and retail.

Finance Industry: Digital transformation has revolutionized the finance industry, enabling financial institutions to streamline their operations, enhance customer experience, and innovate their service offerings. One of the key areas where digital transformation has made a significant impact is in banking and payments. With the advent of online banking, mobile banking, and digital payment solutions, customers can now perform transactions anytime, anywhere, without the need to visit a physical bank branch. This has not only improved convenience for customers but has also resulted in operational efficiency for banks by reducing the need for physical infrastructure and personnel.

Digital transformation has also enabled financial institutions to leverage data analytics and artificial intelligence (AI) to gain valuable insights into customer behavior, risk assessment, and fraud detection. Advanced data analytics tools allow financial institutions to analyze large volumes of data in real-time, identify patterns and trends, and make data-driven decisions.

This has helped financial institutions to personalize their offerings, provide targeted recommendations, and improve risk management, resulting in enhanced customer satisfaction and reduced risk exposure.

Furthermore, digital transformation has also led to the emergence of financial technology (fintech) companies that are disrupting traditional financial services by leveraging innovative technologies. Fintech companies are able to quickly adapt to changing market dynamics, offer agile and customer-centric solutions, and drive innovation in areas such as peer-to-peer lending, robo-advisory, and blockchain-based solutions. Traditional financial institutions are also embracing digital transformation to collaborate with fintech companies, creating new business models and partnerships that drive innovation in the industry.

Healthcare Industry: The healthcare industry has been significantly impacted by digital transformation, leading to improved patient outcomes, increased operational efficiency, and enhanced innovation in healthcare services. Digital transformation has facilitated the adoption of electronic health records (EHRs), telehealth, and remote monitoring, enabling healthcare providers to access patient information, collaborate, and provide care remotely. This has improved patient access to healthcare services, especially in remote or underserved areas, and has resulted in reduced healthcare costs, increased patient engagement, and improved patient outcomes.

Digital transformation has also facilitated the use of data analytics and AI in healthcare, leading to more accurate diagnoses, personalized treatment plans, and improved patient care. Advanced analytics tools can analyze large volumes of healthcare data, such as patient records, medical imaging, and genomic data, to identify patterns and trends that can aid in early disease detection, treatment optimization, and predictive analytics. AI-powered tools, such as machine learning algorithms, can continuously learn from data and provide insights that can assist healthcare providers in making informed decisions and delivering personalized care.

In addition, digital transformation has also facilitated the development of innovative healthcare solutions, such as wearable devices, telemedicine platforms, and digital therapeutics. These solutions enable patients to monitor their health, receive remote consultations, and access virtual care from the comfort of their own homes. Moreover, digital transformation has also accelerated the development of personalized medicine, precision medicine, and genomics-based therapies, which have the potential to revolutionize the treatment of diseases and improve patient outcomes.

Manufacturing Industry: Digital transformation has brought significant changes to the manufacturing industry, leading to increased agility, efficiency, and innovation in manufacturing processes. Digital technologies, such as the Internet of Things (IoT), cloud computing, and robotics, have enabled manufacturers to connect and automate their processes, leading to improved operational efficiency, reduced costs, and increased product quality.

IoT has enabled manufacturers to collect data from connected devices, such as sensors and machines, and analyze the data in real-time to gain insights into the performance of their manufacturing processes. This allows for predictive maintenance, optimized resource allocation, and improved production scheduling, resulting in reduced downtime and increased productivity. Cloud computing has also enabled manufacturers to store and analyze large volumes of data, facilitating data-driven decision-making and enabling remote monitoring and management of manufacturing operations. Robotics and automation have further enhanced agility in manufacturing by reducing human errors, increasing production speed, and enabling flexible production lines that can quickly adapt to changing demand.

Digital transformation has also enabled manufacturers to leverage advanced analytics and AI to optimize their supply chain operations. Manufacturers can analyze data from various sources, such as suppliers, customers, and logistics providers, to gain insights into demand patterns, inventory levels, transportation routes, and production capacity. AI algorithms can then analyze this data to optimize supply chain processes, such as demand forecasting, inventory management, and logistics planning, resulting in reduced costs, improved delivery times, and increased customer satisfaction.

Furthermore, digital transformation has facilitated innovation in the manufacturing industry by enabling the development of new business models, such as servitization and product-as-a-service. Manufacturers are now offering not only products but also services, such as maintenance, repairs, and upgrades, as part of their value proposition. This has resulted in increased customer loyalty, improved customer relationships, and new revenue streams. Additionally, digital technologies have enabled the customization and personalization of products, allowing manufacturers to offer tailored products to individual customers, resulting in increased customer satisfaction and brand loyalty.

Retail Industry: Digital transformation has disrupted the traditional retail industry, leading to increased agility, innovation, and customer engagement. E-commerce has revolutionized the retail landscape, enabling customers to shop online, access a wide range of products, and receive products at their doorstep. This has resulted in increased convenience for customers, expanded market reach for retailers, and reduced costs associated with physical stores.

Furthermore, digital transformation has enabled retailers to leverage data analytics and AI to gain insights into customer behavior, preferences, and purchasing patterns. Retailers can analyze customer data from various sources, such as online and offline transactions, social media, and loyalty programs, to create personalized offers, recommendations, and promotions. This has resulted in improved customer segmentation, targeted marketing campaigns, and increased customer loyalty.

In addition, digital transformation has facilitated the integration of online and offline retail channels, creating an omnichannel retail experience for customers. Customers can now shop online and pick up products in-store, return online purchases in-store, or order products online and have them delivered to their preferred location. This seamless integration of online and offline channels has resulted in increased customer convenience, improved customer experience, and increased customer loyalty.

Moreover, digital transformation has enabled retailers to leverage technologies such as augmented reality (AR) and virtual reality (VR) to enhance the shopping experience. Customers can now virtually try on clothes, visualize furniture in their homes, and experience products in a virtual environment, leading to improved customer engagement, reduced returns, and increased sales.

Digital transformation has also facilitated innovation in the retail industry by enabling the development of new business models, such as subscription-based services, online marketplaces, and direct-to-consumer (D2C) channels. Retailers are now able to sell products and services directly to customers through their own online platforms, bypassing traditional distribution channels, and gaining better control over the customer experience and pricing. This has led to increased innovation in product offerings, pricing models, and customer engagement strategies.

Digital transformation is driving agility and innovation across various industries, including finance, healthcare, manufacturing, and retail. Organizations that embrace digital transformation are able to leverage advanced technologies such as data analytics, AI, IoT, cloud computing, and robotics to streamline their operations, improve customer experience, and create new business models. Digital transformation has resulted in increased agility in adapting to changing market dynamics,

6.7 Competitive Advantage

Ultimately, digital transformation can provide organizations with a competitive advantage in the marketplace. By leveraging digital technologies, organizations can create new business models, develop innovative products and services, and gain insights that can give them a unique advantage over their competitors.

Digital transformation can lead to competitive advantage by enabling companies to adopt new technologies and business models that enhance their operational efficiency, customer engagement, and innovation capabilities.

One way digital transformation can provide a competitive advantage is by optimizing business processes through automation and data-driven decision-making. By leveraging technologies such as artificial intelligence and machine learning, companies can streamline their operations, reduce costs, and improve productivity. For example, predictive analytics can help companies identify potential operational issues before they arise, enabling them to take proactive measures to prevent them from occurring.

Digital transformation can also enhance customer engagement and satisfaction, leading to increased loyalty and revenue. By leveraging digital channels such as social media, mobile apps, and chatbots, companies can deliver personalized experiences that meet the needs and preferences of individual customers. Additionally, digital transformation can enable companies to collect and analyze customer data, providing insights that can inform the development of new products and services.

Innovation is another area where digital transformation can provide a competitive advantage. By adopting agile development methodologies and leveraging emerging technologies such as the Internet of Things (IoT), companies can quickly prototype and test new ideas and bring them to market faster than their competitors. Additionally, digital transformation can enable companies to collaborate more effectively with partners and customers, leading to new business models and revenue streams.

Overall, digital transformation can provide a competitive advantage in several ways, including:

1. Improved operational efficiency - Digital transformation can automate and optimize business processes, reducing costs and improving productivity.
2. Enhanced customer engagement - Digital transformation can enable companies to deliver personalized experiences that meet the needs and preferences of individual customers, leading to increased loyalty and revenue.
3. Increased innovation - Digital transformation can enable companies to quickly prototype and test new ideas, collaborate more effectively with partners and customers, and bring new products and services to market faster than their competitors.
4. Data-driven decision-making - Digital transformation can provide companies with real-time insights into their operations and customers, enabling them to make more informed decisions that drive growth and profitability.

In today's rapidly evolving business environment, digital transformation is no longer an option but a necessity. Companies that embrace digital transformation can gain a significant competitive advantage over their peers by improving operational efficiency, enhancing customer engagement, and driving innovation. By leveraging emerging technologies and adopting new business models, companies can position themselves for long-term success in an increasingly digital world.

Digital transformation is critical for modern businesses to remain competitive and relevant in today's fast-paced business world. By embracing digital technologies, organizations can improve efficiency, enhance customer experience, become more agile and innovative, and ultimately gain a competitive advantage.

Chapter 7: Digital Transformation Pitfalls and Challenges

7.1 The Problem of Lack of Clear Strategy and Goals for Digital Transformation

One of the most significant potential pitfalls of digital transformation is a lack of clear strategy and vision. Organizations that embark on digital transformation without a clear understanding of their goals and objectives may end up investing in technologies that do not align with their business needs. This can lead to wasted resources, poor user adoption, and ultimately, failure to achieve the desired outcomes.

Another potential pitfall is a lack of leadership and culture change. Digital transformation is not just about implementing new technologies; it also involves a cultural shift within the organization to embrace new ways of working, collaboration, and decision-making. This shift requires strong leadership and a willingness to take risks, experiment, and learn from failures.

Data privacy and security are also potential pitfalls of digital transformation. As organizations collect and analyze more data, there is a greater risk of data breaches and cyber-attacks. Organizations must take steps to ensure that they have robust data privacy and security measures in place to protect sensitive information.

To avoid these and other potential pitfalls, organizations must develop a clear strategy and vision for digital transformation, with a focus on aligning technology investments with business needs. Strong leadership is also critical, with leaders who are willing to take risks, experiment, and learn from failures.

Organizations must also prioritize data privacy and security, implementing robust measures to protect sensitive information. This requires collaboration between IT and business leaders, as well as an understanding of regulatory requirements and industry best practices.

In the following chapters, I will delve deeper into these and other potential pitfalls of digital transformation, and provide practical guidance on how to avoid them. I will also examine case studies of both successful and unsuccessful digital transformations, providing real-world examples of what works and what doesn't in digital transformation. Ultimately, our goal is to help organizations navigate the complex world of digital transformation and emerge as leaders in the fast-paced digital economy.

Digital transformation can be a complex and daunting undertaking for organizations of all sizes. While there are many benefits to digital transformation, organizations must approach it with a clear strategy and goals in mind to achieve success.

One of the most significant potential pitfalls of digital transformation is a lack of clear strategy and goals. Organizations that embark on digital transformation without a clear understanding of their objectives may end up investing in technologies that do not align with their business needs. This can lead to wasted resources, poor user adoption, and ultimately, failure to achieve the desired outcomes.

Without clear goals and objectives, it can be challenging to measure the success of digital transformation initiatives. Organizations must have a clear understanding of what they hope to achieve through digital transformation, and how they will measure progress towards those goals. It is important to remember one cannot control what one does not measure. Without this clarity, it is challenging to make informed decisions about technology investments and prioritize initiatives effectively.

Another issue that arises from a lack of clear strategy and goals is a lack of buy-in from stakeholders. When organizations do not have a clear understanding of the objectives of digital transformation, it can be difficult to get buy-in from stakeholders, including employees, customers, and partners. This lack of buy-in can hinder progress towards digital transformation goals and create resistance to change within the organization.

The Importance of a Clear Strategy and Goals

Having a clear strategy and goals for digital transformation is essential for organizations to achieve success. A clear strategy helps to align technology investments with business needs, ensuring that organizations are investing in the right technologies to achieve their objectives.

Clear goals also enable organizations to measure progress towards achieving their digital transformation objectives. This provides a framework for making informed decisions about technology investments and prioritizing initiatives effectively.

Finally, having a clear strategy and goals for digital transformation can help to get buy-in from stakeholders. When stakeholders understand the objectives of digital transformation and how they will benefit from it, they are more likely to support it and work towards its success.

7.2 Resistance to Change from Employees

One of the biggest challenges organizations face during digital transformation is resistance to change from employees. This resistance can be caused by various factors, such as fear of job loss, lack of understanding of new technologies, and reluctance to learn new skills. Overcoming this resistance is crucial for digital transformation initiatives to succeed.

The Problem of Resistance to Change

Resistance to change from employees can hinder digital transformation initiatives in several ways. For instance, it can slow down the implementation process, lead to poor adoption of new technologies, and ultimately, impact the success of the initiative. Resistance to change can also lead to increased costs and wasted resources, as organizations may have to spend more time and money to convince employees to embrace new technologies.

Resistance to change can also create a negative work culture, where employees feel frustrated and disengaged. This can impact productivity, employee morale, and customer satisfaction.

The Importance of Addressing Resistance to Change

Addressing resistance to change is critical for the success of digital transformation initiatives. By overcoming resistance to change, organizations can accelerate the implementation process, reduce costs, and increase adoption of new technologies. Addressing resistance to change can also help create a positive work culture, where employees feel empowered and motivated to embrace new technologies.

7.3 Failure to Consider the Impact on Customer Experience

Digital transformation initiatives can have a significant impact on the customer experience. However, if organizations fail to consider the impact on the customer experience, it can lead to negative consequences. In this section, I will discuss the importance of considering the impact on the customer experience during digital transformation initiatives.

The Problem of Failure to Consider the Impact on Customer Experience

One of the biggest pitfalls of digital transformation is the failure to consider the impact on the customer experience. This can happen when organizations focus solely on the technology or internal processes without considering how it will impact the customer. Experience has shown that due to a lack of education regarding technology available to improve customer experience, most organization focus primarily on internal process digitization and as such lose out on the opportunity to improve their customers' experience. This can lead to a negative customer experience, resulting in reduced customer satisfaction and loyalty.

The Importance of Considering the Impact on Customer Experience

Considering the impact on the customer experience is crucial for the success of digital transformation initiatives. By considering the impact on the customer experience, organizations can:

- Improve customer satisfaction and loyalty
- Increase customer retention and acquisition
- Enhance brand reputation
- Increase revenue and profitability

7.4 Overreliance on Technology

Technology is a critical component of digital transformation. However, organizations can fall into the trap of overreliance on technology, which can lead to negative consequences. In this section, I will discuss the problem of overreliance on technology during digital transformation initiatives.

The Problem of Overreliance on Technology

Overreliance on technology can lead to several negative consequences during digital transformation initiatives, including:

- Lack of focus on the customer experience
- Neglect of critical business processes
- Unnecessary complexity and cost
- Increased risk of security breaches and data loss
- Limited flexibility and scalability

The Importance of Balancing Technology with Business Needs

Balancing technology with business needs is critical for the success of digital transformation initiatives. By balancing technology with business needs, organizations can:

- Ensure that the focus remains on the customer experience
- Ensure that critical business processes are not neglected
- Minimize unnecessary complexity and cost
- Reduce the risk of security breaches and data loss
- Increase flexibility and scalability

7.5 Underestimating the Costs and Time Involved

Digital transformation initiatives can be costly and time-consuming, and organizations can fall into the trap of underestimating the costs and time involved. In this section, I will discuss the problem of underestimating the costs and time involved during digital transformation initiatives.

The Problem of Underestimating the Costs and Time Involved

One of the biggest pitfalls of digital transformation is underestimating the costs and time involved. This can happen when organizations fail to conduct a thorough analysis of the costs and time required for the initiative, resulting in inaccurate budget and timeline estimates. This can lead to budget overruns, missed deadlines, and reduced return on investment.

The Importance of Accurate Cost and Time Estimates

Accurate cost and time estimates are critical for the success of digital transformation initiatives. By accurately estimating the costs and time required, organizations can:

- Develop realistic budgets and timelines
- Ensure that the initiative is financially viable
- Manage stakeholder expectations

- Minimize the risk of budget overruns and missed deadlines
- Maximize the return on investment

The digital transformation journey can be complex and challenging, requiring organizations to invest significant time, effort, and resources to achieve their desired outcomes. However, it is not uncommon for the cost and time of digital transformation initiatives to be underestimated. In this expert article, I will explore the reasons behind this phenomenon and shed light on the potential consequences of underestimating the cost and time of digital transformation efforts.

Digital transformation involves leveraging digital technologies to fundamentally change how organizations operate, deliver value to customers, and achieve their strategic objectives. It encompasses various aspects, such as business processes, organizational culture, customer experience, and technology infrastructure. Organizations often embark on digital transformation initiatives with the expectation of achieving benefits such as improved efficiency, increased innovation, enhanced customer experience, and sustainable competitive advantage. However, the complexity and scale of digital transformation can present challenges that may lead to underestimating the cost and time required for successful implementation.

One of the main reasons why the cost and time of digital transformation are often underestimated is the inherent complexity and interdependencies of the various components involved. Digital transformation is not a one-size-fits-all approach, and each organization's journey is unique. It requires a comprehensive understanding of the existing processes, systems, and culture within the organization, as well as the external factors such as industry regulations, market dynamics, and customer expectations. Many organizations underestimate the complexity of integrating new technologies with their existing legacy systems, data sources, and processes, which can result in unforeseen challenges and delays.

Another factor contributing to underestimation is the rapidly evolving nature of technology. Technology advancements happen at an unprecedented pace, and organizations may struggle to keep up with the latest trends, capabilities, and best practices. New technologies may require significant investment in infrastructure, software, and training, and organizations may not anticipate the full cost and time implications accurately. Moreover, technology implementation can also be accompanied by a learning curve for employees, which may impact productivity and increase the time required for adoption.

In addition, digital transformation often involves significant changes in organizational culture and mindset. It requires organizations to embrace a digital-first mindset, encourage innovation, and foster a culture of continuous learning and adaptation. However, changing the mindset and culture of an organization is not an overnight process and can take time. Organizations may underestimate the effort required to shift the culture and mindset of employees, which can impact the pace and success of digital transformation efforts.

Organizational change management is another critical aspect that is often overlooked or underestimated in digital transformation initiatives. Change management involves addressing the human side of digital transformation, including communication, training, stakeholder engagement, and resistance management. Organizations may not fully appreciate the need for robust change management strategies and the resources required to effectively manage the change process. This can result in resistance from employees, delays in adoption, and overall project inefficiencies.

Moreover, budget constraints can also contribute to the underestimation of the cost and time of digital transformation. Organizations may set unrealistic budgets for digital transformation initiatives, resulting in inadequate resources for implementation, testing, and optimization. This can lead to cost overruns, delays, and compromises on the quality of the implementation.

The consequences of underestimating the cost and time of digital transformation can be detrimental to organizations. Some of the potential consequences include:

1. Cost overruns: Underestimating the cost of digital transformation can lead to budget constraints and cost overruns. Organizations may face unexpected expenses related to technology implementation, infrastructure upgrades, employee training, and change management efforts. This can strain the financial resources of the organization and impact its ability to achieve the expected return on investment (ROI) from the digital transformation initiative.

2. Delays in implementation: Digital transformation initiatives may be delayed due to unforeseen challenges and complexities. Underestimating the time required for various tasks, such as technology implementation, data migration, process re-engineering, change management, and employee training, can lead to delays in the overall implementation timeline. This can result in missed

opportunities, increased competition, and potential loss of market share.

3. Reduced quality of implementation: When organizations underestimate the cost and time of digital transformation, they may be forced to make compromises on the quality of implementation. This can result in rushed deployments, inadequate testing, and suboptimal configurations, leading to potential issues, such as system failures, data breaches, and operational inefficiencies. Poor quality implementation can undermine the intended benefits of digital transformation and result in costly rework or fixes in the future.

4. Employee resistance and low adoption: Change can be challenging for employees, and underestimating the effort required for change management can result in employee resistance to digital transformation efforts. This can lead to low adoption rates, lack of enthusiasm, and even pushback against the initiative. Employee resistance can hinder the success of digital transformation, as the full potential of the new technologies and processes may not be realized if employees are not fully onboard and engaged.

5. Missed opportunities for innovation: Digital transformation is often driven by the need to stay competitive and innovative in today's rapidly changing business environment. Underestimating the cost and time of digital transformation can result in missed opportunities for innovation. Organizations may not be able to invest in the latest technologies, explore new business models, or respond to emerging market trends, leading to potential loss of competitive advantage.

6. Reputational damage: Organizations that fail to deliver on their digital transformation initiatives may face reputational damage. Customers, partners, and stakeholders may perceive the organization as lacking in innovation and responsiveness to market changes. This can impact the organization's brand image, customer trust, and overall market position.

To mitigate the risk of underestimating the cost and time of digital transformation, organizations can take several proactive measures:

1. Comprehensive planning: Organizations should invest adequate time and effort in comprehensive planning before embarking on a digital transformation initiative. This includes conducting a thorough assessment of

current processes, systems, and culture, as well as understanding the external factors that may impact the initiative. Organizations should create a detailed roadmap with realistic timelines, budgets, and milestones, and regularly review and update the plan throughout the project.

2. Robust change management: Change management should be an integral part of any digital transformation initiative. Organizations should invest in robust change management strategies, including communication, stakeholder engagement, training, and resistance management. This will help ensure that employees are fully engaged and supportive of the digital transformation efforts, reducing the risk of resistance and low adoption.

3. Accurate budgeting: Organizations should accurately estimate the budget required for digital transformation initiatives, considering all the aspects, such as technology implementation, infrastructure upgrades, employee training, and change management efforts. It is important to allocate adequate resources to avoid budget constraints and cost overruns.

4. Agility and flexibility: Organizations should adopt an agile and flexible approach to digital transformation,

allowing for adjustments and iterations as needed. This includes being open to changing requirements, emerging technologies, and market dynamics. Agile methodologies, such as Scrum or Kanban, can be employed to facilitate flexibility and adaptability throughout the digital transformation journey.

5. Technology expertise: Organizations should seek external expertise when needed to ensure a successful digital transformation. This may include partnering with experienced technology providers, consultants, or specialists to leverage their knowledge, skills, and best practices. Technology experts can provide insights, guidance, and support in implementing complex technologies and mitigating risks.

6. Continuous monitoring and evaluation: Organizations should establish a robust monitoring and evaluation framework to track the progress of the digital transformation initiative. This includes regular reviews of the implementation status, milestones, budget, and outcomes. Any deviations from the plan should be addressed promptly to avoid potential delays or issues.

Digital transformation is a complex and multifaceted process that requires careful planning, execution, and monitoring. Underestimating the cost and time of digital transformation can lead to various challenges and risks, including cost overruns, project delays, reduced quality of implementation, employee resistance, missed opportunities for innovation, and reputational damage. To mitigate these risks, organizations should adopt a proactive approach, including comprehensive planning, robust change management, accurate budgeting, agility and flexibility, technology expertise, and continuous monitoring and evaluation.

Comprehensive planning involves conducting a thorough assessment of current processes, systems, and culture, and creating a detailed roadmap with realistic timelines, budgets, and milestones. Organizations should also consider external factors, such as regulatory compliance, market trends, and customer demands, in their planning process. Regular reviews and updates to the plan throughout the project can help ensure alignment with changing business needs.

Robust change management is crucial to address the human side of digital transformation. Organizations should invest in effective communication, stakeholder engagement, training, and resistance management to ensure that employees are fully engaged and supportive of the digital transformation efforts. This can help mitigate employee resistance and low adoption rates, and ensure a smoother transition to new technologies and processes.

Accurate budgeting is essential to avoid cost overruns and budget constraints during digital transformation. Organizations should carefully estimate the budget required for all aspects of the initiative, including technology implementation, infrastructure upgrades, employee training, and change management efforts. It is important to allocate adequate resources and regularly monitor the budget to ensure that it remains on track.

Agility and flexibility are critical in the fast-paced and dynamic environment of digital transformation. Organizations should be open to changing requirements, emerging technologies, and market dynamics. Agile methodologies, such as Scrum or Kanban, can be employed to facilitate flexibility and adaptability throughout the digital transformation journey. This allows organizations to quickly respond to changes and make necessary adjustments to the initiative.

Technology expertise is crucial to successfully implement complex technologies and mitigate risks during digital transformation. Organizations should leverage external expertise, such as technology providers, consultants, or specialists, to gain insights, guidance, and support. Technology experts can help organizations make informed decisions, avoid common pitfalls, and ensure smooth implementation of digital transformation initiatives.

Continuous monitoring and evaluation are essential to track the progress of digital transformation and address any deviations from the plan. Organizations should establish a robust framework to monitor and evaluate the implementation status, milestones, budget, and outcomes. Regular reviews and corrective actions can help organizations identify and address issues early on, minimizing the risk of delays or failures.

In addition to these proactive measures, organizations should also foster a culture of innovation, adaptability, and continuous improvement to support successful digital transformation efforts. This includes encouraging experimentation, learning from failures, and rewarding innovation. It is also important to involve employees at all levels in the digital transformation journey, making them feel ownership and accountability for the initiative.

In conclusion, underestimating the cost and time of digital transformation can pose significant challenges and risks for organizations. However, with comprehensive planning, robust change management, accurate budgeting, agility and flexibility, technology expertise, continuous monitoring and evaluation, and a culture of innovation, organizations can mitigate these risks and ensure successful digital transformation. Organizations should approach digital transformation with a strategic mindset, recognizing it as a complex and ongoing process that requires careful management, collaboration, and adaptability. By doing so, organizations can leverage the full potential of digital technologies to drive agility, innovation, and competitive advantage in today's fast-changing business landscape.

7.6 Data Privacy and Security Concerns

Digital transformation initiatives often involve the collection, storage, and processing of sensitive data, and organizations can fall into the trap of neglecting data privacy and security concerns. In this section, I will discuss the importance of data privacy and security during digital transformation initiatives.

The Problem of Neglecting Data Privacy and Security Concerns

Neglecting data privacy and security concerns during digital transformation initiatives can lead to several negative consequences, including:

1. Data breaches: If data privacy and security measures are not properly implemented during the digital transformation project, the organization's sensitive information may be exposed to unauthorized individuals or cybercriminals, leading to data breaches.

2. Legal and regulatory compliance: Organizations may be subject to legal and regulatory compliance requirements related to data privacy and security. Neglecting these requirements during a digital transformation project may result in legal and financial penalties, as well as damage to the organization's reputation.

3. Loss of trust: Customers, partners, and stakeholders may lose trust in the organization if their personal data is compromised or mishandled during a digital transformation project. This can damage the organization's reputation and impact its long-term success.

4. Business continuity: Data breaches and other security incidents can disrupt the organization's operations, leading to downtime, lost productivity, and revenue loss.

5. Intellectual property theft: Neglecting data privacy and security during a digital transformation project can lead to the theft of intellectual property, such as trade secrets, patents, and proprietary information.

The Importance of Data Privacy and Security

Data privacy and security are critical for the success of digital transformation initiatives. By ensuring that data privacy and security are a priority, organizations can mitigate the above risks.

7.7 Insufficient Change Management

Digital transformation often involves significant changes to an organization's processes, systems, and culture, and requires effective change management to ensure success. Change management refers to the process of planning, implementing, and managing change in an organization, with the goal of minimizing disruption and maximizing the adoption and benefits of the change. Here are some key considerations for change management during digital transformation:

1. Communicate the vision and strategy: Leaders should communicate a clear and compelling vision of the digital transformation, including the benefits and goals of the project, to all stakeholders in the organization. This helps build support and understanding for the change.

2. Involve stakeholders: Involve stakeholders from across the organization in the digital transformation project, including employees, customers, and partners. This

helps build buy-in and engagement, and ensures that the digital transformation is aligned with the organization's goals and needs.

3. Assess impact and risks: Conduct a thorough assessment of the impact and risks of the digital transformation, including how it will affect the organization's people, processes, and technology. This helps identify potential roadblocks and areas that require special attention.

4. Develop a change management plan: Develop a comprehensive change management plan that includes timelines, milestones, and responsibilities for all stakeholders. This helps ensure that the digital transformation is implemented smoothly and that any issues are addressed quickly.

5. Provide training and support: Provide training and support for employees to help them adapt to the changes brought about by the digital transformation. This can include training on new technology, processes, and procedures, as well as providing ongoing support and resources to help employees navigate the changes.

6. Monitor and adjust: Monitor the progress of the digital transformation and be prepared to adjust the change management plan as needed. This helps ensure that the

digital transformation is successful and that any issues or concerns are addressed in a timely manner.

By implementing these key considerations, organizations can effectively manage change during a digital transformation and ensure the success of the project.

7.8 Lack of Employee Training and Development

Digital transformation initiatives require employees to adapt to new technologies, processes, and ways of working, and organizations can fall into the trap of neglecting employee training and development. In this section, I will discuss the importance of employee training and development during digital transformation initiatives.

The Problem of Neglecting Employee Training and Development

Neglecting employee training and development during digital transformation initiatives can lead to several negative consequences, including:

- Resistance to change from employees
- Decreased productivity and efficiency
- Increased risk of errors and mistakes
- Reduced employee engagement and job satisfaction

The Importance of Employee Training and Development

Employee training and development are critical for the success of digital transformation initiatives. By ensuring that employees are properly trained and developed, organizations can:

- Increase employee understanding and adoption of new technologies, processes, and ways of working
- Maximize productivity and efficiency
- Minimize the risk of errors and mistakes
- Improve employee engagement and job satisfaction

Chapter 8: Examples of Companies That Failed to Successfully Transform Digitally

Digital transformation is a challenging and complex process, and not all companies have been successful in their efforts. In this chapter, I will discuss some examples of companies that have failed to successfully transform digitally.

A well-known photographic company that was once a major player in the industry but failed to adapt to the shift towards digital photography, ultimately leading to its bankruptcy in 2012. This company had already developed a digital camera in the 1970s, which indicates that they had early knowledge of the emerging digital photography trend. However, despite this early investment, the company did not put enough resources into developing digital technology further, and continued to rely heavily on their traditional film business.

This lack of investment and adaptation to changing technology trends proved to be the downfall of the company. As the digital photography industry grew rapidly, with the emergence of smartphones and other digital devices, the company struggled to keep up and lost its market share to competitors who had invested more heavily in digital technology.

As a result, the company was unable to remain profitable and eventually declared bankruptcy in 2012. This serves as a cautionary tale for businesses that fail to adapt to changing technologies and trends in their industries, as it can have severe consequences for their long-term success and survival.

A practical example of how a lack of clear strategy and goals for digital transformation can lead to failure is the case of what was once a large international video/DVD rental company. It once was a dominant player in the video rental industry, with thousands of stores across the United States and around the world. However, the rise of digital streaming services such as Netflix and the shift towards digital content consumption caught the company off guard. Despite making some initial efforts to transition to a digital model, they failed to develop a clear strategy and goals for digital transformation, leading to its eventual demise.

The company failed to understand the importance of digital transformation and how it would impact their business model. They did not anticipate the shift towards digital content and did not invest in developing a clear strategy and goals to adapt to the changing market. As a result, they lost their competitive advantage and were unable to keep up with the changing consumer preferences.

Their lack of clear strategy and goals for digital transformation led to several missteps that ultimately contributed to their failure. For example, the company tried to launch a streaming service in 2008, but it was too little, too late, and failed to gain traction. Additionally, the company invested heavily in expanding its brick-and-mortar stores, while failing to invest in digital channels or develop a strategy to compete with emerging digital players. They went bankrupt in 2010.

In contrast, Netflix developed a clear strategy and goals for digital transformation, which allowed them to successfully pivot from a DVD rental service to a digital streaming platform. They understood the importance of investing in technology and digital channels, and developed a customer-centric approach that focused on delivering personalized content to their subscribers. As a result, Netflix was able to disrupt the video rental industry and become a dominant player in the digital streaming market.

The failure of the company highlights the importance of developing a clear strategy and goals for digital transformation. Companies that fail to adapt to the changing market and invest in new technologies and business models risk being left behind by their competitors.

A large international retail brand was once a retail giant but struggled to keep up with the shift towards e-commerce. The company did not invest enough in its online presence and was slow to adapt to changing consumer preferences. As a result, it declared bankruptcy in 2018. The statement refers to a large international retail brand that was once a retail giant but struggled to keep up with the shift towards e-commerce. E-commerce refers to the buying and selling of goods or services through the internet, typically through online marketplaces or websites. As consumer preferences shifted towards the convenience of online shopping, this retail brand failed to invest enough in its online presence. This lack of investment and adaptation to changing consumer preferences proved to be a significant challenge for the company. While competitors invested heavily in e-commerce, this retail brand was slow to adapt and failed to keep pace with the competition. As a result, the company lost market share and struggled to remain profitable, ultimately leading to its bankruptcy in 2018. This example highlights the importance of staying ahead of changing consumer preferences and investing in emerging technologies and platforms. In today's digital age, businesses must continually adapt to the rapidly changing technological landscape to remain competitive and successful. Failure to do so can result in losing market share and ultimately, bankruptcy.

8.1 Analysis of the Reasons for Their Failure

There are several reasons why companies fail to successfully transform digitally. In this section, I will analyze the reasons for the failures of the companies discussed in the previous section.

1. Lack of Vision and Strategy: One of the main reasons why all three of these companies failed to transform digitally was a lack of vision and strategy. These companies did not have a clear understanding of how digital technology would impact their industries and did not develop a comprehensive strategy to adapt to the changing landscape.

2. Failure to Innovate: Another reason for the failure of these companies was a failure to innovate. They did not invest enough in research and development or in developing new products and services to meet the changing needs of their customers. One of the big considerations with digital transformation, is not to only follow a "me too" approach, but to invest some money in R&D and innovation.

3. Resistance to Change: Resistance to change was also a significant factor in the failure of these companies. They were slow to adopt new technologies and processes and

did not invest enough in employee training and development.

Chapter 9: Lessons Learned from These Failures

Despite their failures, there are several lessons that can be learned from the experiences of these 3 companies. In this chapter, I will discuss some of these lessons.

1. Embrace Change: Companies must be willing to embrace change and adapt to the shifting landscape of their industries. They must be proactive in identifying emerging trends and technologies and develop strategies to stay ahead of the curve.

2. Invest in Innovation: Companies must invest in innovation to stay competitive. They must be willing to take risks and develop new products and services to meet the changing needs of their customers.

3. Develop a Comprehensive Strategy: Companies must develop a comprehensive strategy for digital transformation that includes a clear vision, goals, and a roadmap for implementation. This strategy must be communicated effectively to all stakeholders to ensure buy-in and support.

These examples of companies that failed at digital transformation illustrate the challenges and complexities of digital transformation. Their failures highlight the importance of developing a comprehensive strategy, embracing change, investing in innovation, and addressing resistance to change. By learning from these failures, other companies can avoid the same pitfalls and successfully transform digitally to remain competitive and relevant in their industries.

9.1 How to Develop a Clear Digital Transformation Strategy, Goals and Roadmap

Here are more detailed steps on how to develop a clear strategy and goals for digital transformation:

1. Conduct a Needs Assessment: Start by conducting a needs assessment to understand your organization's current state, challenges, and opportunities. This will help you identify the key areas where digital transformation can have the biggest impact and provide direction for your strategy.

2. Identify Goals and Objectives: Based on your needs assessment, identify specific goals and objectives for your digital transformation. These goals should be measurable, achievable, and aligned with your overall business strategy. Examples of digital transformation goals could include improving customer experience, increasing operational efficiency, or expanding into new markets.

3. Analyze Your Data: Analyze your data to identify areas where digital technology can be applied to improve your operations, reduce costs, or increase revenue. This could include using machine learning to optimize your supply chain, implementing automation to streamline processes, or leveraging data analytics to gain insights into customer behavior.

4. Identify Key Performance Indicators (KPIs): Once you have identified your goals and objectives, identify the key performance indicators (KPIs) that will help you measure progress and success. These KPIs should be specific, measurable, and aligned with your goals. Examples of KPIs could include customer satisfaction ratings, revenue growth, or employee productivity metrics.

5. Develop a Roadmap: Based on your goals, objectives, and KPIs, develop a detailed roadmap for your digital transformation. This should include specific initiatives, timelines, and milestones for achieving your goals. Your roadmap should also identify the resources and budget required to execute your plan.

6. Prioritize Your Initiatives: Prioritize your initiatives based on their potential impact and feasibility. This will help you focus your resources on the initiatives that will

deliver the most value in the shortest amount of time. You may also want to consider the level of risk associated with each initiative and develop contingency plans in case of unexpected challenges.

7. Communicate Your Strategy: Communicate your digital transformation strategy and goals to all stakeholders in your organization. This includes employees, customers, vendors, and investors. Make sure that everyone understands the objectives, benefits, and timeline of your plan.

8. Monitor and Adjust your Roadmap: Monitor progress towards your goals on a regular basis and adjust your strategy as necessary. Use your KPIs to track performance and identify areas that require improvement. Make adjustments to your roadmap as needed to ensure that you stay on track towards your digital transformation goals.

9. Be Agile in your approach to Digital transformation, innovate, test, discover. Be ready to change direction on a moment's notice and do not only follow a "me too" approach.

By following these steps, you can develop a clear strategy and goals for digital transformation that align with your business objectives and drive meaningful results.

9.2 Achieving Employee Buy-In, Involvement and Commitment

Here are more detailed steps on how to get employee buy-in and involvement during digital transformation:

1. Start with a Vision: Clearly articulate the vision and goals of the digital transformation initiative. This should include the benefits that the organization hopes to achieve through the implementation of new digital tools and processes. This will help employees understand the why behind the initiative and become invested in its success.

2. Identify the Stakeholders: Identify the key stakeholders who will be impacted by the digital transformation. This includes employees who will be using the new technology, managers who will be responsible for leading their teams through the change, and other internal and external stakeholders. Consider their perspectives, interests, and concerns when developing your communication and engagement strategy.

3. Communicate Early and Often: Start communicating about the digital transformation initiative early in the planning process, and continue to provide updates and progress reports throughout the implementation. Use multiple channels, including company-wide emails, town

hall meetings, and individual meetings with employees to ensure that everyone has the opportunity to hear about the initiative and ask questions.

4. Involve Employees in the Planning Process: Involve employees in the planning process by seeking their input on the specific tools and processes that should be implemented. This can be done through surveys, focus groups, or other methods of collecting feedback. This will help to ensure that the digital transformation is designed with the needs and preferences of employees in mind, and that they feel invested in the outcomes.

5. Provide Training and Support: Provide training and support to employees to ensure that they are equipped to use the new technology and processes effectively. This can include classroom training, online resources, and ongoing support through a help desk or other support channels. Encourage employees to ask questions and seek help when needed.

6. Empower Employees to Lead Change: Empower employees to lead change by providing opportunities for them to take ownership of the digital transformation initiative. This can include assigning them to lead teams or working groups, giving them the opportunity to

experiment with new technology, or providing recognition and rewards for their contributions.

7. Celebrate Successes and Address Challenges: Celebrate successes and address challenges as they arise throughout the digital transformation initiative. This can include recognizing teams or individuals who have successfully adopted new tools or processes, and addressing any issues or concerns that are raised by employees. This will help to maintain momentum and encourage continued engagement throughout the initiative.

By following these steps, you can get employee buy-in and involvement during digital transformation. This will help to create a culture of innovation and continuous improvement, and ensure that the initiative is successful in achieving its goals.

9.3 Prioritizing Customer Experience

Customer experience is a critical factor in the success of digital transformation. In this section, I will discuss the importance of prioritizing customer experience.

1. Understanding Customer Needs: Understanding the needs and expectations of customers is essential to providing a positive customer experience. This can be

achieved by conducting customer research, analyzing feedback, and using customer data to inform decision-making.

2. Personalization: Personalizing the customer experience can help to build loyalty and increase customer satisfaction. This can be achieved by using customer data to deliver personalized content and offers.

9.4 How to Balance Technology with Human Expertise

Balancing technology with human expertise during digital transformation is critical to achieving the best outcomes. Here are some detailed steps on how to achieve this balance:

1. Identify Critical Processes: Identify the business processes that are most critical to the organization's success. This will help you determine where technology can provide the most value and where human expertise is most needed.

2. Evaluate Technology Options: Evaluate the technology options that are available for each critical process. Consider the benefits and limitations of each option, as well as the costs and feasibility of implementation.

3. Involve Employees: Involve employees in the selection and implementation of new technology. This can include seeking their input on which tools will be most effective, providing training and support to help them use the new technology, and providing opportunities for them to provide feedback on the process.

4. Define Roles and Responsibilities: Clearly define the roles and responsibilities of both technology and human expertise in the critical processes. This will help to

ensure that everyone understands their role in the process and can work together effectively.

5. Monitor Performance: Monitor the performance of the critical processes after implementing new technology to ensure that the desired outcomes are being achieved. This can include tracking metrics such as productivity, efficiency, and customer satisfaction.

6. Provide Feedback: Provide feedback to employees on their performance and how their expertise is contributing to the success of the organization. This can include recognition and rewards for their contributions, as well as opportunities for career development.

7. Continuously Improve: Continuously improve the technology and processes used in critical processes based on feedback from employees and performance metrics. This will help to ensure that the organization is always using the most effective tools and processes to achieve its goals.

By following these steps, you can balance technology with human expertise during digital transformation. This will help to ensure that the organization is able to leverage the benefits of new technology while also tapping into the expertise and creativity of its employees.

9.5 How to Accurately Estimate Costs and Time

Here are some detailed steps on how to achieve accurate estimation:

1. Define the Scope: Clearly define the scope of the digital transformation initiative. This includes identifying the specific business processes, technology, and organizational functions that will be impacted by the initiative.

2. Develop a Plan: Develop a detailed plan for the digital transformation initiative, including timelines, milestones, and dependencies. This will help to ensure that all stakeholders understand what needs to be done and when.

3. Identify Resources: Identify the resources that will be needed to complete the digital transformation initiative. This includes human resources, technology resources, and other resources such as training and support.

4. Estimate Costs: Estimate the costs of the digital transformation initiative based on the resources that will be needed. This should include direct costs such as hardware and software, as well as indirect costs such as training and support.

5. Identify Risks: Identify the risks that may impact the cost and timeline of the digital transformation initiative. This includes risks such as technology failures, employee resistance, and unexpected delays.

6. Develop Contingency Plans: Develop contingency plans to address the risks identified in step 5. This may include developing alternative plans for completing critical processes, or identifying additional resources that can be brought in if needed.

7. Monitor Progress: Monitor progress throughout the digital transformation initiative to ensure that it stays on track. This includes tracking progress against the plan, identifying any delays or cost overruns, and taking corrective action as needed.

8. Review and Adjust: Regularly review and adjust the cost and timeline estimates based on actual progress and any changes in scope or resources.

By following these steps, you can accurately estimate the costs and time required for digital transformation. This will help to ensure that the initiative stays within budget and timeline, and that the desired outcomes are achieved.

9.6 How to Prioritize Data Privacy and Security

Ensuring the prioritization of data privacy and security during a digital transformation project is essential to protecting sensitive information and maintaining customer trust. Here are some detailed steps on how to achieve this:

1. Identify and Assess Risks: Identify and assess the risks associated with data privacy and security throughout the digital transformation project. This includes assessing the risks associated with data collection, storage, sharing, and processing.

2. Develop Policies and Procedures: Develop and implement policies and procedures that prioritize data privacy and security. This should include policies for data collection, access, sharing, storage, retention, and disposal. Ensure that all employees and stakeholders understand these policies and procedures.

3. Conduct Regular Training: Conduct regular training for employees and stakeholders on data privacy and security best practices. This includes training on how to identify and mitigate risks, as well as on the importance of protecting sensitive information.

4. Implement Security Controls: Implement appropriate security controls to protect sensitive information. This

includes using encryption, firewalls, intrusion detection systems, and other security measures to prevent unauthorized access or breaches.

5. Regularly Review and Update: Regularly review and update policies, procedures, and security controls to ensure that they remain effective and up-to-date with the latest threats and regulations.

6. Conduct Regular Audits: Conduct regular audits of data privacy and security to identify any vulnerabilities or areas of improvement. This includes reviewing access logs, conducting penetration testing, and identifying any potential risks.

7. Maintain Compliance: Ensure that the digital transformation project remains compliant with applicable data privacy and security regulations, such as GDPR or HIPAA. This includes maintaining appropriate documentation and reporting any breaches or incidents.

By following these steps, you can ensure that data privacy and security are prioritized throughout the digital transformation project. This will help to protect sensitive information and maintain customer trust, while also complying with applicable regulations.

9.7 How to Invest in Employee Training and Development

Investing in employee training and development during digital transformation is essential to ensure that your workforce has the necessary skills and knowledge to adopt new technologies and processes. Here are some detailed steps on how to achieve this:

1. Identify Skills Gaps: Identify the skills gaps that exist within your workforce that need to be addressed to support the digital transformation initiative. This may include technical skills, such as programming or data analysis, as well as soft skills, such as communication or leadership.

2. Develop a Training Plan: Develop a comprehensive training plan that addresses the identified skills gaps. This should include specific goals and objectives, as well as a timeline for completing the training.

3. Use a Variety of Training Methods: Use a variety of training methods to ensure that the training is effective and engaging. This may include instructor-led training, online courses, on-the-job training, or mentoring and coaching.

4. Provide Ongoing Support: Provide ongoing support to employees as they learn new skills and technologies.

This may include providing access to resources such as online tutorials or training materials, or providing regular check-ins and feedback.

5. Encourage Collaboration: Encourage collaboration and knowledge sharing among employees to help them learn from each other and share best practices. This may include creating opportunities for employees to work together on projects or establishing online forums or chat groups for discussion and collaboration.

6. Measure and Evaluate: Measure and evaluate the effectiveness of the training program on an ongoing basis. This includes tracking employee progress and performance, as well as collecting feedback from employees to identify areas for improvement.

7. Make Training a Priority: Make employee training and development a priority within the organization by allocating sufficient resources and providing support from leadership. This helps to create a culture of continuous learning and development that supports the digital transformation initiative.

Chapter 10: Digital Transformation and Change Management

In today's fast-paced business environment, digital transformation has become a critical undertaking for organizations of all sizes and industries. The rapid advancement of technology has disrupted traditional business models and created new opportunities for growth and innovation. However, digital transformation is not just about adopting new technologies; it also requires significant changes in the way organizations operate, their processes, and their people. Managing these changes effectively through change management is crucial for the success of any digital transformation initiative.

Change management is the discipline that focuses on guiding individuals, teams, and organizations through the process of change to achieve desired outcomes. It involves planning, implementing, and monitoring changes to ensure they are effectively integrated into the organization's culture, processes, and operations. Change management is particularly important during digital transformation because it helps organizations navigate the challenges and complexities associated with adopting new technologies and digital ways of working.

One of the key reasons why change management is crucial during digital transformation is that it helps organizations mitigate the risks associated with change. Change can be disruptive and unsettling for employees, as it challenges their established ways of working and introduces uncertainty about the future. Change management helps organizations proactively identify and address potential risks and challenges, such as resistance to change, loss of productivity, and employee disengagement. By developing a comprehensive change management strategy, organizations can anticipate and manage these risks effectively, minimizing their impact on the overall success of the digital transformation initiative.

Another important aspect of change management during digital transformation is that it ensures that the organization's people are ready and prepared for the changes ahead. Digital transformation often involves significant shifts in job roles, skills requirements, and work processes. Employees may need to learn new skills, adapt to new tools and technologies, and adopt new ways of working. Change management helps organizations identify the skills and capabilities required for the digital transformation and provides the necessary training and support to enable employees to acquire these skills. This helps ensure that the workforce is prepared for the changes and can effectively contribute to the success of the digital transformation initiative.

Furthermore, change management during digital transformation helps organizations build a culture that is conducive to change and innovation. In today's digital age, organizations need to be agile and adaptable to thrive in the competitive business landscape. Change management promotes a culture of continuous improvement, learning, and innovation, where employees are encouraged to embrace change as an opportunity for growth and development. It also fosters open communication, collaboration, and feedback, which are essential for driving successful digital transformation initiatives. A supportive and inclusive culture that values and embraces change is critical for creating an environment where employees feel empowered and motivated to embrace digital transformation and drive innovation across the organization.

Change management also plays a crucial role in ensuring that the organization's processes and operations are aligned with the digital transformation goals. Digital transformation often involves reevaluating and redesigning business processes to leverage the full potential of digital technologies. Change management helps organizations assess their existing processes and identify areas that need improvement or reengineering to align with the digital transformation objectives. It also facilitates the implementation of new processes and workflows and helps employees understand and adapt to these changes. This ensures that the organization's operations are optimized for the digital age, and resources are effectively utilized to achieve the desired outcomes of the digital transformation initiative.

Moreover, change management during digital transformation helps organizations manage the expectations of various stakeholders. Digital transformation initiatives typically involve multiple stakeholders, including employees, customers, partners, and shareholders. Each stakeholder group may have different expectations, concerns, and needs related to the digital transformation initiative. Change management helps organizations effectively communicate the purpose, goals, and benefits of the digital transformation initiative to different stakeholder groups. It also facilitates ongoing communication and engagement with stakeholders to address their concerns, provide updates on the progress of the digital transformation, and solicit feedback. Managing stakeholder expectations is crucial for building trust, maintaining support, and securing buy-in for the digital transformation initiative, which is essential for its success.

Another significant aspect of change management during digital transformation is the ability to adapt to changing circumstances and unforeseen challenges. Digital transformation initiatives can be complex and dynamic, and organizations need to be prepared to adjust their plans and strategies as needed. Change management provides the flexibility and agility to respond to unexpected obstacles, changes in the business environment, or shifts in technology trends. It helps organizations anticipate potential roadblocks and develop contingency plans to minimize disruptions and keep the digital transformation initiative on track.

Additionally, change management during digital transformation enables organizations to maximize the return on investment (ROI) from their digital initiatives. Digital transformation initiatives often require significant investments in technology, infrastructure, and resources. To ensure a positive ROI, organizations need to effectively manage the changes associated with the digital transformation to realize the intended benefits. Change management helps organizations identify and measure the key performance indicators (KPIs) that are aligned with the digital transformation objectives. It also monitors and evaluates the progress of the digital transformation initiative against these KPIs and identifies areas that may require adjustments or improvements to optimize the ROI from the digital transformation investment.

Furthermore, change management during digital transformation promotes a proactive approach to change, rather than a reactive one. Instead of simply reacting to changes as they occur, organizations can take a proactive approach by anticipating and planning for changes in advance. Change management enables organizations to assess the impact of the digital transformation on their people, processes, and operations and develop strategies to effectively manage these changes. This proactive approach helps organizations minimize disruptions, reduce resistance to change, and achieve a smoother and more successful digital transformation.

Change management during digital transformation also promotes innovation and creativity within organizations. Digital transformation is not just about adopting new technologies; it also requires organizations to think differently and embrace innovative ways of working. Change management encourages employees to think critically, challenge the status quo, and come up with creative solutions to problems. It fosters a culture of experimentation and learning, where employees feel empowered to try new things, learn from failures, and iterate on ideas. This culture of innovation is essential for organizations to stay competitive in the digital era and continuously adapt to the changing business landscape.

Moreover, change management during digital transformation helps organizations build resilience and adaptability to change. In today's rapidly changing business environment, organizations need to be agile and adaptable to respond to market shifts, customer demands, and technology disruptions. Change management develops the necessary skills, capabilities, and mindset within the organization to navigate change effectively. It helps employees develop resilience to cope with the challenges and uncertainties associated with change and adaptability to embrace new ways of working. This resilience and adaptability are critical for organizations to remain agile and competitive in the face of digital disruption.

In addition, change management during digital transformation promotes employee engagement and ownership. Employees are the drivers of change within organizations, and their commitment and involvement are crucial for the success of any change initiative. Change management engages employees in the digital transformation process from the early stages, involving them in the planning, design, and implementation of the changes. This empowers employees to take ownership of the changes and become champions of the digital transformation initiative. When employees are engaged and feel valued as part of the change process, they are more likely to embrace the changes, become advocates for the digital transformation initiative, and contribute to its success.

Furthermore, change management during digital transformation helps organizations build a positive employer brand and attract top talent. In today's competitive job market, organizations need to differentiate themselves as attractive employers to attract and retain the best talent. Digital transformation is often associated with innovation, growth, and opportunities for career advancement, and organizations that effectively manage change during digital transformation are perceived as forward-thinking and progressive employers. A positive employer brand not only helps organizations attract top talent but also boosts employee morale, engagement, and productivity. Change management ensures that employees are equipped with the necessary skills, knowledge, and support to embrace the changes associated with digital transformation. This creates a positive work environment where employees feel valued, supported, and motivated to contribute their best efforts towards the success of the digital transformation initiative.

Moreover, change management during digital transformation helps organizations manage and mitigate risks. Digital transformation initiatives can introduce various risks, such as disruptions to business operations, potential data breaches, changes in regulatory compliance, and resistance from employees or other stakeholders. Change management identifies, assesses, and mitigates these risks through careful planning, communication, and stakeholder engagement. It helps organizations develop risk management strategies and contingency plans to minimize the impact of risks on the digital transformation initiative. By effectively managing risks, organizations can ensure a smooth and successful digital transformation journey with minimal disruptions and setbacks.

Another important aspect of change management during digital transformation is stakeholder management. Digital transformation initiatives often impact various stakeholders, including employees, customers, partners, suppliers, and other external stakeholders. Change management helps organizations identify and engage these stakeholders, understand their needs and concerns, and communicate the benefits of the digital transformation initiative to them. It ensures that stakeholders are informed, involved, and supportive of the changes, which is critical for their acceptance and cooperation. Effective stakeholder management fosters trust, collaboration, and alignment among stakeholders, which can significantly contribute to the success of the digital transformation initiative.

Furthermore, change management during digital transformation promotes organizational learning and continuous improvement. Digital transformation is a complex and dynamic process that requires organizations to continuously learn, adapt, and improve their strategies, processes, and capabilities. Change management facilitates the process of learning from experiences, successes, and failures throughout the digital transformation journey. It encourages organizations to reflect on their progress, gather feedback, and make necessary adjustments to optimize the outcomes of the digital transformation initiative. This culture of continuous improvement helps organizations evolve and stay ahead in the ever-changing digital landscape.

Lastly, change management during digital transformation fosters long-term sustainability. Digital transformation is not a one-time event but an ongoing process that requires organizations to continuously evolve and innovate to remain relevant and competitive. Change management ensures that the changes associated with digital transformation are embedded into the organization's culture, processes, and operations in a sustainable manner. It promotes a mindset of continuous change and adaptability, which enables organizations to thrive in the digital age. It also ensures that the benefits and outcomes of the digital transformation initiative are sustained over the long term, rather than fading away after the initial implementation.

In conclusion, change management is of paramount importance during digital transformation initiatives. It ensures that organizations effectively manage the people, process, and cultural changes associated with digital transformation, and maximize the success of the initiative. Change management provides a structured approach to plan, implement, and monitor the changes, and enables organizations to anticipate and address potential challenges and risks. It fosters a culture of innovation, adaptability, and continuous improvement, and engages employees and stakeholders in the digital transformation process. Moreover, change management during digital transformation promotes resilience, agility, and sustainability, which are crucial for organizations to thrive in the rapidly changing digital landscape. Therefore, organizations undertaking digital transformation initiatives must prioritize change management to ensure a smooth, successful, and sustainable digital transformation journey.

Chapter 11: Importance of careful planning and execution

In this chapter, I will discuss the importance of careful planning and execution in ensuring successful digital transformation. I will explain how companies must approach digital transformation with a clear strategy that outlines specific goals and objectives. I will discuss the importance of involving all stakeholders in the planning process, including employees, customers, and partners. Additionally, I will explore the significance of regularly evaluating progress, adjusting plans as necessary, and ensuring effective communication across all levels of the organization.

Digital transformation has become an imperative for businesses across all industries. It entails the integration of digital technologies into all aspects of a company's operations, from customer experience and marketing to supply chain management and workforce collaboration. However, successful digital transformation requires careful planning and execution to reap its full benefits.

One of the key reasons why planning is crucial for digital transformation is because it helps organizations define their objectives and align their strategies accordingly. Companies need to identify their digital goals and understand how technology can help them achieve these goals. Planning also involves identifying potential risks and challenges that may arise during the implementation process, allowing businesses to develop mitigation strategies to address these issues proactively.

Execution is equally important for digital transformation, as it involves putting the plans into action. Effective execution requires collaboration among different teams and departments, as well as the allocation of resources and the implementation of best practices. Organizations must also be willing to adapt to changes and make necessary adjustments along the way.

Successful digital transformation can bring numerous benefits to businesses, such as increased efficiency, improved customer experience, and enhanced competitiveness. However, these benefits can only be realized through careful planning and execution. Companies that prioritize these aspects of digital transformation are more likely to achieve their objectives and maintain their competitive edge in the ever-evolving digital landscape.

Digital transformation is a complex process that involves integrating digital technologies into all aspects of a business. For a digital transformation to be successful, it is essential to involve all stakeholders in the planning process, including employees, customers, and partners.

Employees are one of the most critical stakeholders in the digital transformation process. They are the ones who will be using the new digital technologies, and their buy-in is crucial for successful implementation. Involving employees in the planning process ensures that their input is considered and that they have a sense of ownership in the project. This can lead to greater adoption of new digital tools and technologies, resulting in increased efficiency and productivity.

Customers are another vital stakeholder in digital transformation. They are the ones who will be using the products or services that are being transformed. By involving customers in the planning process, businesses can gain valuable insights into their needs and preferences. This can help businesses develop more customer-centric strategies and products, resulting in increased customer satisfaction and loyalty.

Partners are also essential stakeholders in digital transformation. They can provide valuable expertise and resources to support the implementation of new technologies. By involving partners in the planning process, businesses can ensure that they have the necessary support and collaboration to make the transformation a success.

Involving all stakeholders in the planning process of digital transformation is essential for success. It helps to ensure that everyone is aligned and invested in the project and that the transformation is customer-centric, employee-focused, and supported by partners. By taking a collaborative approach to digital transformation planning, businesses can increase the likelihood of achieving their goals and staying competitive in the digital age.

Digital transformation is a continuous process that requires regular evaluation of progress, adjustment of plans, and effective communication across all levels of an organization. Here are some reasons why:

Regular evaluation of progress is critical to ensure that digital transformation initiatives are on track to achieve their objectives. Without regular assessments, it's challenging to identify what's working, what's not, and where improvements can be made. Regular progress evaluations allow businesses to measure their success and identify areas that need improvement. This can help businesses stay on track and make necessary adjustments to ensure that the digital transformation initiatives are successful.

Adjusting plans as necessary is also critical to successful digital transformation. Business environments are dynamic, and unforeseen events can affect the implementation of digital transformation initiatives. Regularly reviewing and adjusting plans can help businesses adapt to these changes and stay on course. This can help businesses remain flexible and agile, which is crucial for success in today's digital age.

Effective communication across all levels of an organization is also essential for successful digital transformation. Digital transformation affects everyone in the organization, from senior executives to front-line employees. Effective communication ensures that everyone is aware of what's happening, what the goals are, and how the digital transformation initiatives will impact them. It helps to build trust and ensures that everyone is on the same page. Effective communication also allows for feedback, which can help businesses make necessary adjustments and ensure that digital transformation initiatives are successful.

Regularly evaluating progress, adjusting plans as necessary, and ensuring effective communication across all levels of the organization are crucial for successful digital transformation. It helps businesses stay on track, adapt to changes, and ensures that everyone is aligned and invested in the process. By taking these steps, businesses can increase the likelihood of achieving their goals and staying competitive in the digital age.

Chapter 12: Conclusion

If you are planning to start your digital transformation journey, I wish you all the best and hope that these pointers and guidelines will help your transformation journey be a great success. If you have already started your journey and have encountered some of these pitfalls and obstacles, I hope that this guide will help you overcome those obstacles.